Introduction

Before you dismiss this book as just another work trying to convince Christians to place themselves "back under the Law"; please at least read the Introduction and the Author's Note. There are a multitude of misconceptions within the religion of Christianity, having 38,000+ denominations, each with their own idea or version of the Truth. Can they all be right? This book will be touching on several misconceptions and common questions that are found among believers who call themselves "Christian" when it comes to their view of those who keep the Law.

Prior to this book, I have written two other books. The first book, "Restoring the Path: Examining the Way of the Messiah", was to show that we, in fact, are supposed to keep the Law (Torah). The second book, "Shalom in Fear: Yirah, Sh'ma, Shalom", was to teach us "Godly Fear", wherein, if we were to have this fear in our walk with the Almighty and His Son, we would not mistranslate the Scriptures.

In this book, I attempt to untwist the man-made doctrines that have been keeping believers from understanding the reason we keep the Torah/Law by answering each question individually. I also attempt to provide an excellent tool for believers who do keep the Commands of Elohim (God) so that if and when they are asked why they keep the Torah, observe the Feasts and keep the Sabbath, they can refer back to this book for easy references or hand it to those who ask. It is by no means a substitute for the Scriptures themselves, but it is a tool to point people BACK to the Scriptures as I believe was Yeshua's (and every other Prophet's) message; Teshuva! Return!

So while you start to read the following chapters, keep your heart open to the Ruach HaKodesh/Holy Spirit and allow our Father to teach you through His Son, Yeshua, the Truth that the deaf have not heard and blind have not seen.

"Whoever has ears, let them hear."

-Yeshua (Matthew/Mattiyahu) 11:15)

Author's Greetings

Shalom (Peace). My name is Michael. How are you today? I hope you are well. Let me share a little bit about myself with you before we continue.

I was born and raised as a Pentecostal Christian. I attended Sunday church and as I grew older became very involved in my youth group as a teenager. I would run the sound system, play bass guitar and drums in the worship band. I also attended several trips to conferences held by popular preachers and bands.

Eventually, by the age of 15, I started to seriously study and teach the Bible. That's right! I would stand on the stage in front of all my peers and teach the things I had studied. I also took over as a Children's Church pastor at age 18.

I got married at 21 years old and became a Youth Pastor. I was also involved in a band that played at different churches and Christian functions. I was a Youth Pastor for two and a half years. My wife and I had a child and had to retire from the Youth Ministry due to a strain on our finances, but I continued being a part of the band until we all went our separate ways. I also had weekly Bible studies in my home for a time.

Then, a friend I had gone to church with as a youth (though they were an elder to me) started a Bible Study group that I started attending.   Then something radical happened.

My whole understanding of Scripture was completely changed forever.   The one thing that set me off was being challenged on the keeping of the Seventh-Day Sabbath.   It rattled me so much, the fact that I was wrong on this one matter, that I took an entire year away from church and teachers to study the Scriptures for myself.   If I was wrong about this, what else was I wrong about?

What I had found - without studying with other voices in my head - was shocking to me.   It kept me up at night.   I struggled for the first few months to the point I realized that almost everything I had been taught and was teaching was wrong. I finally submitted to the Will of the Father and started observing the Torah.

After all of this, I started to meet with my friend and the Bible Study group again, where everyone had been calling it the Sabbath Midrash.   A lot had changed, but one thing remained: The Truth.

I eventually started recording video teachings online and wrote my first book.   A cousin of mine made a website for me and I started recording Podcasts.   I then wrote a second book and continued growing my ministry and teachings over the years.

I have had many conversations and debates over the Scriptures. All of these things have led me to this third book.

I'm sure you have many questions for those who believe as I do. I want to spend the next pages of this book addressing and answering some of those questions.

Without any further delay... let's begin!

#1. What is "the Torah"?

The word "Torah" is actually a Hebrew word that is usually translated in most Bibles as "The Law." More accurately, it means "Instructions." In Hebrew, it is spelled תורה (Tav-Vav-Resh-Hey, read from right to left). It is recognized as the first five books of the Scriptures inspired by God and written by Moshe (Moses).

When Moshe heard the voice of God (יהוה Yod-Hey-Vav-Hey, The Name of God), which is the inspiration (In-Breathed/God-Breathed), he wrote it down and kept the historical events that happened to the Hebrew people from the Creation and onward documented. These books (or scrolls) are commonly known as Genesis, Exodus, Leviticus, Numbers and Deuteronomy. However, in Hebrew, they are known as Barashit (In the beginning), Shemot (The names), Vayikra (And He called), Bamidbar (In the wilderness) and Devarim (The Words/Spoken Words).

The Torah is known to have many mitzvot (Commandments). While this is true, many commands are repeated more than once in the Torah due to being on separate occasions. For example, many mitzvot/commands were given at Mount Sinai and throughout the book of Leviticus/Vayikra, then, given again after the 40 years in the wilderness to the next generation that would enter the Land promised to them.

Also, not every command was for every person. Some were given to men only while others were given only to women. Some were to children and others to parents. Some were given to priests only while others were for the common person. Finally, some were for every day while others were for specific days.

In a nutshell, the Torah is the Law of God and is also considered to be the Word of God.

#2. Why are you following Jewish Laws when you are not Jewish?

I should counter with, "Why do you think they are Jewish Laws?" It is a common misconception that the "Old Testament" is strictly Jewish. Let me explain.

The term "Jew" comes from "Judah." Judah was the fourth son of Jacob, who later became known as Israel. The Hebrew word for Judah is "Yehudah" (יהודה Yod-Hey-Vav-Dalet-Hey) and it means "Praise."

King David and King Solomon were both from the tribe of Yehudah, as was the Messiah, Jesus, or Yeshua. When Solomon died around 925 BCE (Before the Common Era), there were ten tribes that would not submit to his son Rehoboam as King. From this, the tribes were split into two kingdoms; the Northern Kingdom (Israel) and the Southern Kingdom (Judah/Yehudah). The southern kingdom contained the tribes of Yehudah (Judah) and Benyamin (Benjamin) which can mean either "Son of the south" or "Son of the right hand." There were also some Levites and priests among them. The southern kingdom was focused around Jerusalem (Yerushalem) and the Temple.

In the 5th century BCE, the Assyrian king Sennacherib came against the Northern Kingdom where they were dispersed and exiled. The Southern Kingdom remained (known as the Kingdom of Yehudah) and would come to be known as the Yehudi, or "Jews."

In context to the question, a Jew would only be concerning one tribe of Israel. However, every tribe was at Sinai when the Torah/Law was given, but it was not only the Hebrew people; Gentiles, or "Goyim", were present as well. In Exodus/Shemot 12:38 (NKJV) we read (concerning the time when the Hebrews began their exodus from Egypt), "A mixed multitude went up with them also, and flocks and herd – a great deal of livestock." These were most likely some of the Egyptians who were foreign to the Hebrew people.

Now I will explain the word "Gentile" or "Goyim." Goyim is the plural form of "Goy" (גוי Gimel-Vav-Yod). The pronunciation "Gentile" comes from the Latin word "Gentilis" which, in connection with the Greek word "Genus", refers to a race or tribe. The Hebrew word "Goy" means "foreigner" while "Goyim" means "foreign nations". From a Scriptural perspective, it often refers to any people-group that is outside of Covenant with God.

Avram (Abram, later Avraham/Abraham) was a goy. He was a gentile. He was not born in the Land of Israel, among other Hebrews or in Covenant with God; there were none. This is because he was called to be the first Hebrew. The Hebrew word for "Hebrew" is "Ivrit" or "Avrit" (עברית Ayin-Vet-Resh-Yod-Tav). Translated, it means "to cross over/crossed over". In Genesis/Barashit 12, we read where God calls Avram to leave the country he is in and all of his family and go into a Land that He will show him. He does so, and later in Genesis/Barashit 14 is called an Ivri, from the word Ivar (עבר Ayin-Vet-Resh) meaning "other side." The idea behind it is that Avram was called out of the pagan/foreign nations (Goyim) into a land he would be shown. Because of this, Avram would be known as someone who "crossed over" and was from the "other side." This is not only practical, but is symbolic of every person who does so in their personal life. We are called to be Kadosh/Holy meaning "separate" or "set apart".

For instance, when we who were in our sin, or practiced what was contrary to God's Ways, or Torah/Law, are called out of them and into God's Ways and into Covenant with Him, we are also called Hebrew, or Ivrit, because we "crossed over" and set ourselves apart from the ways of those who are foreign, or separate from God. The Covenant is found in Exodus/Shemot 19:5-6 (KJV) states, "Now if you obey me fully and keep my Covenant, then out of all nations you will be my treasured possession. Although the whole earth is mine, you will be for me a kingdom of priests and a holy nation."

So then, the original question asked will be changed to something else.

#3. Why do you believe the Torah/Law is still for today?

When the Almighty gave us the Torah/Law, He said in Deuteronomy/Devarim that the things He commanded were forever (4:40, 5:29) and that we were not to add or take away from what was commanded (4:2, 12:32). I should also mention that the Torah/Law is considered to be the "Word" of God. In Hebrew, "Word" is "Devar" (דבר Dalet-Vet-Resh). It is primarily used as a spoken word, or a matter. The Torah/Law was first spoken by the mouth of Yah (poetic short-form of The Name of God), then written down by Moshe (Moses). The Word of God, as considered by the people and the Prophets, was and is the Torah/Law. After the writings of the Prophets had been written, they too were considered the Word of God because the Prophets were inspired (in-breathed/God-breathed) and did as commanded. These things were also written, either by their own hand or by a Scribe.

In Psalm/Tehellim 119, considered to be a Psalm of David by many (though, there's no solid proof for this), the Psalmist writes in vs. 44, "and I will keep your Torah always, forever and ever." Some translations say "Word" instead of "Torah", though the Hebrew indicates more accurately to be "Torah". The whole chapter of Psalm/Tehellim 119 is a must read, but I mention this particular chapter because if it was in fact written by David, a man after Yah's own heart (1 Samuel 13:14, Acts 13:22), then it speaks volumes of what Yah's heart is, which I think is very obvious to see, being the obedience of the Torah.

Likewise, in prophetic books, such as Isaiah/Yeshayahu 2:3 and Micah 4:2 it is stated that in a future time people (including goyim/gentiles) will go to Jerusalem/Zion to hear the Torah/Law which comes from the Mountain. This is prophecy; that the Torah will come forth from Zion in the "end of days" as Micah 4:1 states. It would not make sense for the Torah to come to an end, even for a time, if we will be going forth to hear the Torah in Jerusalem in the end of days.

Moving on into the B'rit Chadesha (Renewed Covenant/New Testament), Yeshua taught and practiced observance of the Torah.

For example, in Matthew/Mattiyahu 23:2, Yeshua (Jesus) is found saying, "All things therefore whatever *they* tell you to observe, observe and do…", however, about 28 or more scrolls of Matthew/Mattiyahu have been found that were written in Hebrew and all agree that Yeshua did not say "whatever *they* tell you", rather, "whatever *HE* tells you." In the previous verse it tells us who "he" is. "The Scribes and Pharisees sit in Moshe's

(Moses') seat. All things therefore whatever *HE* (Moshe) tells you to observe, observe and do…"

It is apparent throughout Yeshua's ministry that He was consistently on the bad side of the Pharisees (but not all of them as I will point out later). This is because He would not submit to the rules and regulations they themselves ADDED to the Torah. As for the matter of Moshe's seat; they built a seat out of stone and called it the seat of Moshe by which whoever sat and spoke from it had the authority to make and change laws. Yeshua made a point, speaking of Moshe's seat, by saying that those who sit in this seat were under the authority of whatever Moshe wrote, being the Torah, but also said in the next part, "but don't do their (the Scribes and Pharisees) works; for they say, and don't do."

Another example of the Torah in the end of days is the Judgement, when Yeshua says in Matthew/Mattiyahu 7:21-23 that the only people who were to enter the Kingdom were those who kept the Will of the Father and the ones who would not enter in were the ones who practiced *"LAWLESSNESS"*.

A final example from Yeshua is when He said in Matthew/Mattiyahu 5:19 (CJB), "So whoever disobeys the least of these mitzvot (commands) and teaches others to do so will be called the least in the Kingdom of Heaven. But whoever obeys them and so teaches will be called great in the Kingdom of Heaven."

Following in the book of Acts, we see the Apostles keeping the Feast Days (Acts 2 and 20 – Shavuot/Pentecost, and another in chapter 18). We also see them keeping the Sabbath/Shabbat numerous times throughout Acts (7 recorded times and more than 80 in total calculated according to Acts 18). In Acts 15, they decreed that when dealing with new converts to the Gospel Message that they would be told a few certain commands at the first. Verse 20 states that they be told to, "abstain from pollutions of idols, and from fornication, and from things strangled, and from blood." This is because Moshe (the Torah) is still being preached every Sabbath and it is clearly seen that it was expected that they would continue to learn the Torah weekly, as seen in the next verse.

Now, in the writings of Sha'ul (Paul), he also teaches that the Torah was to be kept. However, Kefa (Peter) explains in 2 Peter/Kefa 3:16 (NIV), "He writes the same way in all his letters, speaking in them of these matters. His letters contain some things that are hard to understand, which ignorant and unstable people distort, as they do the other Scriptures, to their own destruction." Most likely, Kefa is saying that if you think you understand Sha'ul, you don't, and most people distort what he is really saying as they also do to the Scriptures (Tanakh/Old Testament).

So the reason I believe the Torah is still for today is because:

- The Almighty Himself said they were forever.

- The Prophets said they would be in the end of days.

- Yeshua not only kept the Torah, but taught to keep the Torah.

- The Disciples/Apostles continued to keep them after the death and resurrection.

- Sha'ul (Paul), the author of about half the B'rit Chadesha (Renewed Covenant/New Teastament) also taught to keep the Torah.

#4. The Law was given to show us we can't keep it. Why should we try keeping it if no one can?

This question comes, more or less, from Romans 3:20 (ESV) which states, "For by works of the law no human being will be justified in his sight, since through the law comes knowledge of sin" and from Galatians 3. This is by no means an argument for not keeping the Torah but rather an argument against legalism.

The Galatians 3:10-14 passage teaches us that it is by not legalism that we are justified AND that it is not legalistic to be faithful in keeping the Torah/Law. In fact, the passage is quoting directly FROM the Torah! The Law states "You shall not murder"; it does not make it an act of legalism to obey this command, rather, it is to be LEGAL and RIGHT to keep this command. It is, however, legalistic to keep His commands simply because it is a command rather than because it is right and loving to do so.

The Romans 3:20 passage tells us that the Law gives us knowledge of sin. This is the same as saying that the light gives us knowledge of darkness.

We also know that it is NOT impossible to keep the Torah. If you look at Luke 1:5-6 (KJV), we see something very interesting and inspiring about John/Yochanon's parents, "There was in the days of Herod, the king of Judaea, a certain priest named Zacharias, of the course of Abia: and his wife was of the daughters of Aaron, and her name was Elisabeth. And they were both **righteous** before God, walking in **all** the commandments and ordinances of the Lord **blameless**."

If no one can keep the Law perfectly, or blamelessly, how then did these two pull it off? The Torah itself even teaches us, in Deuteronomy/Devarim 30:11-14 (HRB), "For this command which I am commanding you today is **not** too wonderful for you, nor is it too far off. It is not in the heavens that you should say, Who shall go up into the heavens for us, and bring it to us, and cause us to hear it, that we may do it? And it is **not** beyond the sea that you should say, Who shall cross over for us to the region beyond the sea and take it for us, and cause us to hear it, that we may do it? For the Word is very **near** to you, in your mouth and in your heart, that you **may** do it."

The idea that the Law is impossible to keep is simply a myth and a false doctrine of man.

#5. Didn't Paul say the Torah/Law was "nailed to the cross"?

This question is in reference to Colossians 2:14 (NJB) which says, "He has wiped out the record of our debt to the Law, which stood against us; he has destroyed it by nailing it to the cross."

This is actually a common misconception. Too many people read this one verse without reading the context. Context, as I always like to say, is crucial. That's why I like to keep reading because if you do, in this same chapter, in vs. 22, Sha'ul (Paul) tells you exactly *which* law he is talking about; "...According to merely human commandments and doctrines!"

I think in regards to who Sha'ul was, I should touch on his history. Actually, we should go further back before he was born.

Around the year 165 BCE, there was a split in groups that differed in opinion. They were the Pharisees and the Sadducees. The Sadducees believed strictly in the Torah and that there was no resurrection while the Pharisees held to the belief that there was the written Torah AND an oral Torah. They also believed in the Prophets and held to the belief that there would be a resurrection.

The word "Pharisee" comes from the Hebrew word "Perushim" (פרושים Pey-Resh-Vav-Shin-Yod-Mem) which comes from the Hebrew root word "Parash" (פרש Pey-Resh-Shin) which means "to separate". So then, the term "Pharisee" would be to call them the "separated ones". In their beginnings, this was the goal. In fact, their cause started off seemingly noble. But, as history would have it, corruption began to creep its way in and they began to add to the Torah. Eventually, they had so much influence in Jerusalem that many people adhered to their teachings. When Yeshua started His ministry, He always made it a point to either do the opposite of what the Pharisees taught or to teach others not to observe the ways of the Pharisees. This was anything from the ritual/tradition of washing the hands (Matt. 15:2, Luke 7:2) to spitting into dirt to make mud on the Sabbath (Mark 8, John 9). It is also believed that when Yeshua was at a wedding reception (John 2) that the vessels that were used were actually the vessels that were used in a Pharisee water purification ritual. It should be noted though that not all the Pharisees were corrupt and some were even friends with Yeshua; one even providing a tomb for Him after the Crucifixion.

Even to this day, Pharisees are still around and practicing these and many more practices not found in the written Torah. But in relation to Sha'ul, he was raised to be a Pharisee. In fact, he was one all his life. Even after having become a follower of

Yeshua, he still claimed to be a Pharisee. The term "Pharisee" in today's time actually has a pretty negative imagery surrounding it. Many Christians and Torah-observers think of them as nothing more than disobedient people while, at the core of things, they were a noble and truly zealous group that desired purity. I think, personally, that in their attempts to remain pure they simply let things get out of hand. The phrase "give the devil an inch" comes to mind.

As for Sha'ul, he was famous for having sat at the feat of one of the most revered Pharisees of his time named Gamaliel. Sha'ul would go on to be known as a man who far exceeded his own peers. He knew the Torah word for word. In his writings, he is constantly quoting the Torah and using them to teach and to correct those he wrote to. If you read his writings in full context, you can see his absolute adoration, passion and zeal for the written Torah. He expresses his hatred for being a sinful man though knowing what he should be doing, but instead failing to what he would call the "law of sin".

Shaul mentions many laws in his writings such as the "law of sin", the "law of the mind" and the "Law of God". So when he says that the law was "nailed to the cross", he is not talking about the "Law of God", but as he makes it a point to mention in the same chapter, the law that is of "human commandments and doctrines".

In vs. 15 (KJV) he says, "And having spoiled principalities and powers, he made a shew of them openly, triumphing over them in it." We see this same wording again in Ephesians 6:12 (KJV), "For we wrestle not against flesh and blood, but against principalities, against powers, against the rulers of the darkness of this world, against spiritual wickedness in high places."

Many people assume that this is strictly in reference to demons or unclean spirits. This is not entirely true. Though I agree that he mentions them – "spiritual wickedness" – he is also talking about something else. It is what we see in the Pharisee sect, being the powers and principalities in their own ranks where traditions and doctrines of man had crept in. Sha'ul even makes mention that God had triumphed over them. Likewise, however, this is also in relation to the curse of the Torah/Law. The curse is that if you are disobedient to the Torah, you will be placed under the curse of death. This is what it means to be "under the Law"; it is the penalty, or, to be indebted to the Law.

When Yeshua was crucified He "paid the debt", or as Sha'ul puts it, "blotted out what was contrary to us". That debt, of course, is sin. Sin is defined in 1 John 3:4 (NIV), "Everyone who sins breaks the law; in fact, sin is lawlessness." The Pharisees were in sin by breaking the command to not add or take away from the Torah (Deut. 4:2). Likewise, what was against us was not only the added and subtracted laws of the Pharisees, but also the very act of sin itself found in every person. Yeshua took on the curse of sin (death/the penalty) and when He resurrected He conquered death and we again could have relationship with the Father through the Messiah.

So the answer is no, the Law of God was not nailed to the cross.

#6. Weren't some commands changed or done away with?

It is true that certain practices are not done today. Namely, animal sacrifices. But with this truth comes many misconceptions about "change" and the Torah/Law being "done away with". When dealing with this issue, truths get twisted and passages taken out of context. As some things are not done today, many people seem to automatically assume everything else was done away with and whatever the Messiah (or the Apostles) mentioned in the B'rit Chadesha (Renewed Covenant/New Testament) are all that are required. This is simply not true.

I should first start by quoting what Yeshua said in Matthew/Mattiyahu 5:17 (HNV), "Don't think that I came to destroy the Torah or the Prophets. I didn't come to destroy, but to fulfill." For one, this is a common phrase used then and now – "to destroy the Torah" – commonly understood by Rabbis and Pharisees. If one Rabbi disagreed with another on a matter concerning the Torah, he would tell the one he disagreed with that he was "destroying the Torah", meaning to "teach against it". So in this sense, that is what Yeshua was referring to. Likewise, when He said He had come to "fulfill" it, this also is a common term among Rabbis meaning to "teach correctly".

However, there is also another element to it that should be considered. Some translations use the term "do away with" in regards to the Torah/Law. This is also accurate seeing as Yeshua did not come to do away with it. On the contrary, much of His ministry was spent, not only observing the Torah, but calling others to "Teshuva" (תשובה Tav-Shin-Vav-Vet-Hey) meaning to "Repent" or "Return/Turn back to". The question should be asked, "Return to what?" The answer of course is the Ways of Yah - the Torah. When He said "to fulfill", He meant to bring to completion. He also meant to explain it in its full meaning.

For example, as He came to teach how each mitzvot (command) is likewise in fulfillment of the greatest mitzvot, the command to love, He also came to fulfill symbolic events. The Pesach (Passover) is a historical event that took place (Exodus/Shemot 12). But it also is a foreshadowing of something else to happen, being that Yeshua would be our ultimate Pesach Lamb (1 Corinthians 5:7). His crucifixion took place at the exact day and moment of the Pesach sacrifice. This was a fulfillment.

Now moving on to the so-called "changes"; when the Torah was first given, we were also given instructions under the

Levitical Priesthood. The Levites were to take care of all the sacrifices and fire offerings. This was to occur in and around the Temple, or Tabernacle.

When Yeshua came to fulfill the Torah, one of the things he fulfilled was the sacrificial system. He gave/offered His own life as a perfect sacrifice. At the same time, we were placed under the order of the Melchizedek Priesthood. This is a very ancient order that predates the Levitical order. The Levitical order was very important in its time, but we are now under a greater order of the Melchizedek. Yeshua is the High Priest of the order of Melchizedek, which in Hebrew means, "King of Righteousness."

The Levitical Priesthood was in charge of the temple. They are better known as the "Levites." They would perform the fire offerings, sacrifices and were permitted in and around the Temple. The duties were placed in their care.

Yeshua prophesied that the second Temple would be destroyed (Matthew/Mattiyahu 24) and that prophecy came to pass between 68 CE and 70 CE. Since the Temple was no more, the Levitical Priesthood was of no effect anymore. However, 1 Corinthians 6:19 says that our bodies are the Temple within which the Ruach HaKodesh/Holy Spirit abides. Our High Priest, Yeshua, of the order of the Melchizedek Priesthood, maintains and performs all the duties for this Temple and the one in Heaven. You can read more about this in Hebrews 7. The first mention of Melchizedek can be found in Genesis/Barashit 14. There is also a prophecy concerning Yeshua becoming the Melchizedek Priest in Psalm/Tehellim 110.

Within this, it wasn't so much of a "change" as it was "transference" from one authority to another.

Previously, I mentioned that some people tend to believe that what still stands from the Torah/Law is whatever the Messiah (or the Apostles) mentions in the B'rit Chadesha (Renewed Covenant/New Testament). One must consider what this would mean.

Take into consideration the mitzvot/commands to refrain from sexual intercourse with animals (Leviticus/Vayikra 18:23). This is not mentioned in the B'rit Chadesha. I would have to ask if that would make it permissible to do today. Of course the answer would have to be no. But some might say that it would be considered sexual immorality which the B'rit Chadesha does mention refraining from (1 Thessalonians 4:3). But then I would have to ask what the definition of sexual immorality is. The answer can only be defined based on what the Torah gives, which includes refraining from sexual intercourse with animals. So then, we must accept that the Torah is still just as relevant as it is today and come into an understanding that the only "change" that occurred was concerning the Levitical Priesthood.

#7. Doesn't Paul teach that circumcision is now only a matter of the heart?

This question is primarily from Romans 2, however, it does concern several other passages of Sha'ul's (Paul's) writings.

Romans 2:25-29 (NKJV), "For circumcision is indeed profitable if you keep the law; but if you are a breaker of the law, your circumcision has become uncircumcision. Therefore, if an uncircumcised man keeps the righteous requirements of the law, will not his uncircumcision be counted as circumcision? And will not the physically uncircumcised, if he fulfills the law, judge you who, even with your written code and circumcision, are a transgressor of the law? For he is not a Jew who is one outwardly, nor is circumcision that which is outward in the flesh; but he is a Jew who is one inwardly; and circumcision is that of the heart, in the Spirit, not in the letter; whose praise is not from men but from God."

Galatians 5:2 (NIV), "Mark my words! I, Paul, tell you that if you let yourselves be circumcised, Christ will be of no value to you at all."

We also see what seems to be a contradiction between Sha'ul's teachings and his actions:

Galatians 2:3 (NIV), "Yet not even Titus, who was with me, was compelled to be circumcised, even though he was a Greek."

Acts 16:1-3 (NASB), "Paul came also to Derbe and to Lystra. And a disciple was there, named Timothy, the son of a Jewish woman who was a believer, but his father was a Greek, and he was well spoken of by the brethren who were in Lystra and Iconium. Paul wanted this man to go with him; and he took him and circumcised him because of the Jews who were in those parts, for they all knew that his father was a Greek."

So how do we reconcile this? The answer can be found if the context of Galatians 5 is read in full. The key verse is vs. 4 (HNV), "You are alienated from Messiah, you who **desire to be justified by the law**. You have fallen away from grace." This bolded statement is the crux of the entire problem that Sha'ul faced in his time.

It is believed that the letter to the Galatians was written concerning what happened in Acts 15. More specifically, there was a council (or assembly) that had come together to discuss an issue among them in order to come to a conclusion on the matter. In vs. 1 and 5 (HNV) it is stated that the issue was from the Pharisees. In vs. 1 they said, "Unless you are circumcised after the custom of Moses, you can't be saved." In vs. 5 it is stated, "But some of the sect of the Pharisees who believed rose up, saying, 'It is necessary to circumcise them, and to command them to keep the Torah of Moses.'" We see here that it is an issue of Salvation. Kefa (Peter) stood and spoke to them. While speaking, he said in vs. 11, "But we believe that we are saved through the grace of the Lord Yeshua, just as they are." The Pharisees believed that in order to be saved, whether Jew or Goyim (Gentile), they had to be circumcised. Kefa disagrees with this, as does Sha'ul (as we will see). We are not saved by works of the Torah, but by grace.

The conclusion of the matter is stated in vs. 19-21 by Ya'akov (Jacob), "Therefore my judgment is that we don't trouble those from among the Gentiles **who turn to God**, but that we write to them that they abstain from the pollution of idols, from sexual immorality, from what is strangled, and from blood. For Moses from generations of old has in every city those who proclaim him, being read in the synagogues every Sabbath."

As shown in bold, he is speaking of those who turn to God, implying that it is new converts (or new believers). Those who were telling these new believers that they had to be circumcised and keep the whole Torah were unsettling them. It was that as soon as they proclaimed belief and accepted salvation that all of a sudden they were burdened with a large amount of "rules" and it was overwhelming them. In wisdom, we see the matter resolved by saying they would abstain from the aforementioned things while they learned the rest of the Torah and its observances (including circumcision) every Sabbath as it was still being taught.

They were not saying not to circumcise at all; they were saying it was not to be done in order to become saved.

In the next chapter, Sha'ul circumcises Timothy just before ensuring that the message concluded in chapter 15 was understood and being carried out. The question most people have is why he would circumcise Timothy. Timothy's father was a Greek and his mother was a Jewess and the text says that he had a good report said about him in the parts Sha'ul was taking him. So because of the Jews that were there (likely, those who knew Torah), Sha'ul circumcised him. I believe it was for two reasons. The first being because as we are to be Torah-observant in our walks with Messiah, Sha'ul wanted to ensure there was nothing of Timothy that would place doubt in the minds of those they were going to see. So, as instructed by the Torah, he circumcised him so he would be blameless and so they could not sit in judgment of him for not having been circumcised. He would be better received, as would his message to them. The second reason is something Sha'ul says in 1 Corinthians 9:20, "To the Jews I became as a Jew, that I might gain Jews..."

Now concerning Galatians 2 and Titus, Sha'ul says that he did not feel compelled to be circumcised. The reason why is stated in vs. 4, "This was **because of the false brothers** secretly brought in, who stole in to spy out our liberty which we have in

Messiah Yeshua, that they might bring us into bondage." Sha'ul makes mention that these "false brothers" were men of repute. Their status meant nothing to him, but they were highly respected among men in the surrounding area and they would use whatever information they could to prove this life in Messiah as a false one, or, use it to their own advantage in some way.

If we look back at Romans 2, Sha'ul makes mention of the difference between the letter of Law and the Spirit of the Law. This is, in my mind, the MOST crucial aspect to the entire matter in regards to the keeping of the Torah. Remember, Kefa (Peter) said that Sha'ul's letters are hard to understand and many twist his words as they do the Scriptures. So because of this we must make a note to not take what he has written at face value and look at the depth and the context. If you read it once and think, "Makes sense", chances are you are missing what is being said.

Let us examine what is written in 2 Corinthians 3 starting in vs. 2-3, "You (the Corinthians) are our letter, written in our hearts, known and read by all men; being revealed that you are a letter of Messiah, served by us, written not with ink, but with the Spirit of the living God; not in tablets of stone, but in tablets that are hearts of flesh." In this, he is alluding to a prophecy found in Jeremiah/Yirmayahu 31:33, "I will put my law in their minds and write it on their hearts. I will be their God, and they will be my people."

The basis of the Renewed Covenant is that the Torah would be written on our hearts rather than tablets of stone. It was internalized.   In this, we find its strength, not in the Letter, but in the Spirit.

He continues, concerning the Messiah, in vs. 6, "Who also made us sufficient as servants of a new covenant; not of the letter, but of the Spirit. For the letter kills, but the Spirit gives life." This must be understood.   At face value, the average thought is that he is saying that the Torah/Law is what kills.   But remember, Kefa says you are likely wrong.   So what is the difference between the Letter and the Spirit?   It is a matter of the heart. It is not a matter of Salvation.   It is a matter of love.

Take a look at 1 John/Yochanon 5:3 (CJB), "For this is the love of God, that we keep his commandments: and his commandments are not grievous."   Some translations say "are not burdensome".   Also, take a look at James/Ya'akov 2:24 (CJB), "You see that a person is declared righteous because of actions and not because of faith alone."

Salvation comes by grace through Yeshua, but our love and faith is made tangible and real by our actions and obedience. It should be a pleasure to serve and obey His Torah, not a burden. Many of the Psalms declare the Torah to be a joy and liberty to them.

In answer to the original question; the answer is it was a matter of WHY it was being done; in order to become saved or because it was the right thing to do.   Was it because of the

Letter of the Torah (because it was written) or the Spirit of the Torah (why it was written).

Take, for example, the command not to murder. We can do it simply because it is written, "You shall not murder", or we can refrain from murder because it is contrary to showing love to one another which is the sum of the whole Torah. So then, in conclusion, it is simply a matter of the heart. Not to please others, but because it is right and loving toward God to do so.

"For in Messiah Yeshua neither circumcision amounts to anything, nor uncircumcision, but faith working through love."

- Galatians 5:6

#8. Paul said as long as I was convinced in my own mind, any day can be holy. Doesn't this mean the Seventh-Day Sabbath is done away with?

This question is in reference to Romans 14. Sha'ul (Paul) is writing to them about a problem they were having amongst one another concerning days to fast on and food to eat. I know you may read it and ask, "Where does it say fast?" Contextually, the evidence is there, as well as historically. In fairness, I would have to also counter with, "Where does it say Sabbath?"

Sha'ul begins by talking about food (the first evidence). In vs. 3 Sha'ul places instructions for both sides saying, "Don't let him who eats despise him who doesn't eat. Don't let him who doesn't eat judge him who eats, for God has accepted him." One is basically fine with eating meat while the other is not and only eats vegetables. The reason for this is because, as Sha'ul was writing to Jews and Roman converts, the markets among them were full of meat that had been sacrificed to false gods. While one felt it was not a problem and ate unto the Lord, the other felt uneasy about this and would only eat vegetables (similar to Daniel in Babylon). It should also be noted that the Jews at that time were under Roman occupation.

Likewise, while still in the context of food, Sha'ul says in vs. 5-6, "One man esteems one day as more important. Another esteems every day alike. Let each man be fully assured in his own mind. He who observes the day, observes it to the Lord; and he who does not observe the day, to the Lord he does not observe it. He who eats, eats to the Lord, for he gives God thanks. He who doesn't eat, to the Lord he doesn't eat, and gives God thanks." It should also be noted that the Pharisees, who added laws to Torah, had a system in place that a believer would, or should, fast twice weekly (Luke 18:12 according to their custom). The Almighty gives no command for specific days to fast on (other than Yom Kippur/The Day of Atonement) which also caused this conflict.

The issue was not one of whether the Sabbath had been done away with, but that believers were judging one-another based on their own standards. If you have been reading the previous questions, you would know by now that there was great conflict among believers. You would also know that Sha'ul was an advocate, as were his writings, in favor for the Torah and the keeping and observing of its mitzvot/commands. So in context of all of the writings of Sha'ul, we can only conclude that he is not telling us to be comfortable with another day being the Sabbath (contrary to Yah's own Word) or every day being the Sabbath. Remember, the Apostles themselves were documented in the book of Acts to have kept the Sabbath over 80 times.

Sha'ul continues to talk about eating and not eating throughout the chapter. The conclusion on the matter of which day is holiest to fast on and what foods (clean according to Torah) are common or not comes to each believer being convinced in their own minds on the matter and not forcing their beliefs on others and condemning them according to their own standard.

However, we as believers should judge one-another according to the standard of the Torah. Yeshua does this (Matt. 18) as did Sha'ul (1 Tim. 1).

#9. Does Colossians 2 say no one can judge me in food, drink or keeping the Sabbath?

Context, again, is crucial. Let's take a look at Colossians 2:13-17, "You were dead through your trespasses and the uncircumcision of your flesh. He made you alive together with him, having forgiven us all our trespasses, wiping out the handwriting in ordinances which was against us; and he has taken it out of the way, nailing it to the cross; having stripped the principalities and the powers, he made a show of them openly, triumphing over them in it. Let no one therefore judge you in eating, or in drinking, or with respect to a feast day or a new moon or a Sabbath day, which are a shadow of the things to come; but the body is Messiah's."

As we have already discussed; not only are "powers and principalities" related to unclean/demon spirits, but also in this case refer to false religious practices. Again, the Phraisees had in place rules and regulations in addition to the Torah which is in disobedience to the command not to add or subtract from the Torah. Yeshua spent much of His ministry making a spectacle and teaching against the false teachings of the Pharisees. This included additional rules and regulations with their own observances in eating, drinking, Feast Days, New Moon celebrations and Sabbath Days.

For example, the Pharisees have ceremonial regulations in place that commands a person to wash their hands in a special way, with special utensils, while reciting a type of creed. If this is not done, according to their tradition, then one is ritually unclean and therefore the food that they eat is defiled. They have rules also in place about how far a person is allowed to venture away from their home on the Sabbath.

While these rules were added in hopes to keep the people who obeyed them from ever being able to disobey the Torah, they became outrageous, out of hand and ultimately disobedient in and of themselves. Their yolk was a burden, while the Torah, Yeshua's yolk, was light and easy (Matt. 11:29-30, 1 John 5:3).

The wording here, "Let no one therefore judge you in..." is that if you were to keep these mitzvot/commands as instructed by the Almighty and His Son, then no one can be in judgment of you. You are doing it right! Who can judge against you for doing the right thing? No one.

If, however, you are not observing these things as instructed by the Almighty, then a fellow believer has every right to judge you for it because you are in disobedience which is sin.

#10. Yeshua said that what enters the body does not defile it.   Does that mean all things can now be eaten?

This question comes from Matthew/Mattiyahu 15:11 (HNV) which says, "That which enters into the mouth doesn't defile the man; but that which proceeds out of the mouth, this defiles the man."

This was in response to when the Pharisees and scribes came and asked, "Why do your disciples disobey the tradition of the elders?   For they don't wash their hands when they eat bread."   Yeshua's first response was a counter-question, "Why do you also disobey the commandment of God because of your tradition?"   It has been repeated throughout this book that the Pharisees, though they started with good intentions, added to the Torah.   This of course is in disobedience of the mitzvot/command not to add to or subtract from the Torah.

Yeshua continued to answer them by explaining to them how their traditions make the mitzvot/commands of Yah void (due to their additions and subtractions).   The simple answer to this question can be found in vs. 20, "But to eat with unwashed hands doesn't defile the man." THIS is the issue that He was answering. Not that it is the type of food eaten that defiles the man, but whether it is eating with unwashed hands or not.

In the same story, found in Mark 7, it records in the NIV vs. 11, "For it doesn't go into their heart but into their stomach, and then out of the body. (In saying this, Jesus declared all foods clean.)" This has led many people to believe that Yeshua was declaring what the Torah calls "unclean meat" as "clean". There are a few problems with this.

One is that the text here does not say "meats" but "food". The Torah defines what is and is not food. You can find a list of what is considered clean meat in Leviticus/Vayikra 11. It details how to determine what animals may be eaten, as well as what fish may be eaten. The passage also tells how to determine what animals are unclean by the same standards. The Scriptures NEVER say that meat from an unclean animal (such as pig meat) is food, but it rightly admits that it has meat. However, though having meat, it is not considered edible and therefore is not food. So when the text in Mark 7 states "Jesus declared all foods clean", it is right in saying so as food is defined in the Torah. However, it does not mean that all MEAT is clean. It should also be considered that many speculate that the phrase "Jesus declared all foods clean" was added after the original author had written this Gospel because it does not appear in several Greek texts.

Likewise, the CJB gives an extra layer of insight that I consider to be more accurate than other translations by saying

"Thus he declared all foods *ritually* clean."   Since this was only an issue for the Pharisees and their man-made traditions, Yeshua rebutted the entire premise of their practice of the ritual washing of the hands.

In conclusion; no, Yeshua did not declare that we may now eat anything we want.   He was only refuting their rituals.

For more information concerning the topic of clean and unclean meat, please read question #11.

#11. Did Peter's dream in Acts 10 mean that God made all unclean meat clean and good for eating?

The dream Kefa/Peter had in Acts 10:11-16 (HNV) is as follows, "He saw heaven opened and a certain container descending to him, like a great sheet let down by four corners on the earth, in which were all kinds of four-footed animals of the earth, wild animals, reptiles, and birds of the sky. A voice came to him, 'Rise, Peter, kill and eat!' But Peter said, 'Not so, Lord; for I have never eaten anything that is common or unclean.' A voice came to him again the second time, 'What God has cleansed, you must not call unclean.' This was done three times, and immediately the vessel was received up into heaven."

At the first, it does seem to indicate that the voice was telling Shimon (Simon) to go ahead and eat everything present on the sheet. However, Kefa awoke and the passage states, "Now while Peter was very perplexed in himself what the vision which he had seen might mean..." indicating that he knew there was something more to the dream than just what was seen and heard.

Previously, a man named Cornelius who was a Roman Centurion received a vision from the Almighty instructing him to go seek out Shimon Kefa.   He sent three of his men to go.

Afterward, Acts 10 records Kefa's vision.   After the vision, while Kefa was pondering the vision, the Ruach (Spirit) spoke to him and told him the three men were outside looking for him. He met with them and listened to their inquiry and the next day went to meet with Cornelius.   Upon meeting him, he said in vs. 28, "You yourselves know how it is an unlawful thing for a man who is a Jew to join himself or come to one of another nation, but God has shown me that I shouldn't call any man unholy or unclean."   THIS is the meaning of the dream that Kefa had!

The sheet was offered three times and he was told to partake three times.   Three Gentile men (Goyim – Foreigners) came to Kefa and he received them.   As the Jewish law stated (not the Torah), it was unlawful for a Jew to join with a non-Jew. It serves as yet another example of how laws were added. However, the voice in Kefa's dream, whether the voice of the Almighty or the voice of Yeshua, told him, "What God has cleansed, you must not call unclean."   Therefore, the conclusion of this matter is that the dream had absolutely NOTHING to do with food concerning unclean meat being made clean.   It had EVERYTHING to do with Kefa being called to join with the foreigners and not considering them to be unclean anymore.

For more information concerning the topic of clean and unclean meat, please read question #10.

#12. Why would God care about what we eat?

There are several reasons for why the Almighty would care about what we eat.   The reasons, though, are not simply dietary or for health reasons.   They are for spiritual reasons, as well.

To start, I will use an example from Exodus/Shemot 34:26 and Deuteronomy/Devarim 14:21.   There was a command given which stated that we are not to boil a kid in its mother's milk.   A kid, of course, means a young goat.   Many have taken this to mean that we are not to mix dairy with meat, though this is more of a Talmudic teaching and holds no basis or evidence for its interpretation.   The forbidding of this practice is a bizarre command.   In fact, it seems very out of place.

If we look at several commentaries on these passages, as well as historical findings, we find that the practice of boiling or seething a kid in its mother's milk actually has pagan roots.   The Scriptures are very firm in commanding us not to do anything that the pagans do (Deuteronomy/Devarim 12).

In 1929, a library had been found in an archaeological digging site in Syria containing many different writings and tablets whose contents were of literature, myths and religious rituals. On one tablet which was later published in 1933 as "The Birth of the Gracious and Beautiful Gods", there was a damaged line that was restored as best as could be by a man named Charles Virolleaud. As best as could be restored and translated, it contained the words "Cook a kid in milk". This particular listing of rituals was of Canaanite origin and dated to the 14th century BCE.

As it would seem, it appears that in commanding us not to boil a kid in its mother's milk would not necessarily be for our benefit from a dietary standpoint, but to keep us from doing as the pagans do.

On the flip-side, such meat as crow, pig and bottom-feeders in the ocean such as shrimp and crab would be for our health. Many of these animals eat dead and rotting corpses. A pig is already so toxic, even a venomous snake bite wouldn't be able to kill it. It has also been stated before that most if not all influenza viruses come, originally, from pigs. And let's not also forget their own diet that can even contain feces.

I've heard before the argument that in modern times we have ways of purifying the meat in order to make it fit for human consumption. This raises many red flags, though. Does this make it right to break this command? What if the reasons are not only for our own health, but also for spiritual reasons similar to the boiling of the kid in its mother's milk? This could be a dangerous road. It would also be as dangerous as ccepting science over Scripture, though I believe the two go hand-in-hand, but that is another topic.

From my own experience, back when I was transitioning in to a Torah-observant lifestyle, I started to notice a difference in my own state-of-mind between times when I ate Scripturally clean foods and unclean foods. For example, if I had not eaten anything unclean for several days, my dreams at night would be your average types of dreams. But I noticed a few different times, as did my wife, that when we ate Pizza with pepperoni on it (which contained pork), our dreams would be very bizarre. I tested this a few times before I fully committed to eating a strictly clean diet and found that the results were consistent.

I liken this to sea water. I am an avid survival student. I enjoy learning about how to live off the land and build small shelters. One thing that is taught universally when surviving in or around the ocean or sea is to NEVER drink the water. Its salt content is far too potent for human consumption. Those who have done so in past circumstances will often suffer from hallucinations and ultimately death. I believe that these comparisons are worth considering when deciding what should or should not be eaten.

The B'rit Chadesha (Renewed Covenant/New Testament) teaches us that our bodies are the Temple of the Ruach HaKodesh/Holy Spirit. If it was considered an abomination to sacrifice a pig on the altar, or even that one man was allowed in on one day of the year in the Holy of Holies that must be found pure enough to enter, I think it should be deeply and carefully considered what enters our bodies if the Ruach is expected to abide in us.

Nothing our Father does or says is an accident or just for the sake of having fun.   Everything has a purpose to it whether we know it or not.   We cannot and do not see the "big picture" as He does.   We often believe we see everything happening outside just by looking out the window.   But I would bet that the person standing on the roof would see a lot more than the person looking through the window.

Trust in Father and His mitzvot/commands and I believe you will be fine.   Besides, a non-bacon diet never hurt anyone!

#13. Are we saved by works of the Law or by Grace through Yeshua?

This, I believe, is the heart of the matter. Most Christians today believe that those of us who keep the Torah teach that all believers should also teach that it is a matter of salvation. Most often I will hear believers say that they are saved through the blood of Christ and that is all they need; that there is no more need for works of the Law. This answer needs to have your full attention. It is of great importance that this is understood.

First, we will start with salvation. What is it? How are we saved? What are we saved from? Going back to Sinai, we were given mitzvot/commandments together in one Law, or the Torah (Instructions). This was to be the way of life for those who professed living for the Almighty Elohim/God, Yehovah. This was the Covenant made between Yah and His people; that if we were to keep His Commands, He would be our Elohim and bless us (Exodus/Shemot 19). When any person broke a Command or went against the Instructions given, atonement would be required in the form of an animal/blood sacrifice. This would cover their sin.   This was by no means intended to be a permanent covering because each time a person would sin, a new sacrifice was required.

Sin is defined in 1 John/Yochanon 3:4 (NIV), "Everyone who sins breaks the law; in fact, sin is lawlessness."   Yeshua even says in Matthew/Mattiyahu 7:23, "I never knew you; depart from me, you workers of lawlessness," equating Yeshua knowing us with us keeping the Law.   Some translations say "workers of iniquity", taken from the Greek word "Anomia" (ἀνομία) meaning to be in violation of the Law, a transgressor or unrighteous. Literally, it is to be without Instruction or Law.

It is apparent that this causes a great deal of confusion, but if we can understand where our salvation comes from and what it *looks* like to be saved, there can be no more confusion. Yeshua is the prophet that Moshe/Moses spoke of in Deuteronomy/Devarim 18:15 (ESV) when he said, "The LORD your God will raise up for you a prophet like me from among you, from your brothers—it is to him you shall listen."   Yeshua was also prophesied by John/Yochanon to be the "Lamb that takes the world's sin away" (John/Yochanon 1:29).

Other prophecies include:

"He was oppressed and afflicted, yet he did not open his mouth; he was led like a lamb to the slaughter, and as a sheep before its shearers is silent, so he did not open his mouth."

- Isaiah/Yeshayahu 53:7

"Yet it was the LORD's will to crush him and cause him to suffer, and though the LORD makes his life an offering for sin, he will see his offspring and prolong his days, and the will of the LORD will prosper in his hand."

- Isaiah/Yeshayahu 53:10

"On that day a fountain will be opened to the house of David and the inhabitants of Jerusalem, to cleanse them from sin and impurity."

- Zechariah 13:1

Through Yeshua, our sin (lawlessness) was taken away and we were made clean. The Covenant was renewed and the Torah was written on our hearts (Jeremiah/Yirmayahu 31:33, Romans 2:15, Hebrews 10:16).

We who observe the Torah acknowledge that it is only through faith in Yeshua that we are saved, NOT by keeping the Torah. Galatians 2:16 (CJB) says, "We have come to realize that a person is not declared righteous by God on the ground of his legalistic observance of Torah commands, but through the Messiah Yeshua's trusting faithfulness. Therefore, we too have put our trust in Messiah Yeshua and become faithful to him, in order that we might be declared righteous on the ground of the Messiah's trusting faithfulness and not on the ground of our legalistic observance of Torah commands. For on the ground of legalistic observance of Torah commands, no one will be declared righteous." By this, we establish that Salvation is by grace.

This leaves us then with the Law. Why keep it if we are already saved through Yeshua? The reason is very interesting. The reason is "Love".

We will look at 1 John/Yochanon 5:3 (NJB) this time which says, "This is what the love of God is: keeping his commandments. Nor are his commandments burdensome." Yeshua says some things similar to this in John/Yochanon 14:15, "If you love me, you will keep my commands", and in Matthew/Mattiyahu 11:30, "For my yoke is easy, and my burden is light." In Matthew 7:21 (HNV) Yeshua also says, "Not everyone who says to me, 'Lord, Lord,' will enter into the Kingdom of Heaven; but he who does the will of my Father who is in heaven."

For those of us who are saved by grace, there are also things expected of us; how to act, being moral, being obedient and so on. Our morality is defined by the Torah; how we are to dress, worship and even love. The Scriptures tell us that the point of the Torah is to love. By keeping Torah, we show our love for our Father in Heaven. In order to love those around us, the Torah also teaches us this. For example, "You shall not steal". This teaches us how to treat another person's property. "You shall not covet" takes it further by teaching us how not to think or dwell on another person's property or relationships. "You shall not murder" teaches us how to treat another person's life.

The same applies with loving our Father. "You shall have no other gods", which teaches us that loving and having the one true Elohim/God means not having or treating any other gods as you would Him by simply not having any other gods.

"Remember the Sabbath, to keep it kadosh/holy" teaches us to give rest to our bodies (the Temple of the Ruach Kodesh/Holy Spirit) and by remembering the Almighty and all that He has done.

Going outside of the first Ten Commandments, loving ourselves is shown by adhering to the mitzvot/commandments that teach us how to eat (clean meat rather than unclean toxic meat). His Torah also teaches us that keeping His Moedim (Appointed Times/Feast Days) help us to not only draw closer in Echad (Unity/Oneness) with our fellow brothers and sisters, but also to meet with Him and draw closer in relationship with our Father in Heaven.

As I hope you can see, every Instruction given in the Torah is not only for our benefit through His love for us, but also His glory and exaltation. Nothing honors a Father more than an obedient and loving child! It is also still beneficial for every believer today. By having faith in our Creator for sending His Son in grace and mercy to take away our sin and having faith that His Torah is for our benefit in loving one another and Him; we can be found as righteous just as Avraham was and by the blood of Yeshua.

#14. The Torah requires that everyone goes to Jerusalem three times a year. Does this still apply today?

This question is in reference to Exodus/Shemot 23, 34 and Deuteronomy/Devarim 16. These times are during Pesach (Passover) or sometimes referred to as Matzot (Unvleavened Bread), Shavuot (Weeks), and Sukkot (Tents or Booths). These passages state (HNV), "Three times in a year shall all your males appear before the LORD your God in the place which he shall choose: in the feast of unleavened bread, and in the feast of weeks, and in the feast of booths; and they shall not appear before the LORD empty: every man shall give as he is able, according to the blessing of the LORD your God which he has given you."

This is a legitimate concern since following the Torah also means observing the Moedim (Appointed Times/Feasts). Today, Messianics, Hebrew Roots Believers and observant Jews observe these Feasts but are limited in what they can do. Because these Appointed Times were to be observed in Jerusalem with the sacrifices required being carried out at the Temple, it is currently impossible to do these things.

One reason is because the Temple was destroyed sometime between 68CE and 70CE. The other is because the sacrifice of Yeshua was and is a perfect offering so that no animal sacrifice would ever be beneficial again. On this topic, I recommend reading Hebrews 10 in its entirety.

We do still however continue to observe these Appointed Times to the best of our ability. It is also important to note the changing of the Priesthood from the order of the Levitical to the order of the Melchizedek.

More on the orders of the Priesthood can be read in question #6.

In Conclusion

God's Law stands forever.   Not only does Scripture clarify this, but logic as well.   When Daniel refused to eat the unclean food that was offered to him in Babylon, the king's servants became fearful that they will not appear as strong or healthy as they should.   But Daniel challenged them by asking that he only eat vegetables and drink water for 10 days and compare his appearance and ability to the others who did eat the king's food. Daniel 1:15 (ISV) says, "At the end of ten days their appearance was better and their faces were well-nourished compared to the young men who ate the king's rich food."   The Almighty's diet was greater than the king of Babylon's.   Likewise, Daniel and those with him were blessed through their obedience to His Torah/Law, "As for these four young men, God gave them knowledge, aptitude for learning, and wisdom.   Daniel also could understand all kinds of visions and dreams."

If you are still wondering whether you should start observing His Torah, test it!   Not only is it obedience towards our

Father in Heaven, but it reaps benefits and blessings. We may not always understand His plan, but He does in a way we cannot fathom. The Torah gives instructions for health, business, relationships and those who had faith in Him throughout Scripture were brought up to do great and amazing things. But on the other hand, those who disobeyed were no so blessed.

Israel refused to submit to the Sabbath year and God was displeased with this. The reason Daniel was in Babylon was because all Israel were exiled from the Land for not honoring the Sabbath year. The Land was allowed to rest for 70 years - one year for each Sabbath year that was not observed.

Jeremiah/Yirmayahu 25:11-12 (NIV), "'This whole country will become a desolate wasteland, and these nations will serve the king of Babylon seventy years. But when the seventy years are fulfilled, I will punish the king of Babylon and his nation, the land of the Babylonians, for their guilt,' declares the LORD."

Jeremiah/Yirmayahu 29:10 (NIV), "This is what the LORD says: 'When seventy years are completed for Babylon, I will come to you and fulfill my good promise to bring you back to this place.'"

Daniel 9:2 (NIV), "I, Daniel, understood from the Scriptures, according to the word of the LORD given to Jeremiah the prophet, that the desolation of Jerusalem would last seventy years."

2 Chronicles 36:21 (NIV), "The land enjoyed its Sabbath rests; all the time of its desolation it rested, until the seventy years were

completed in fulfillment of the word of the LORD spoken by Jeremiah".

His Torah will be obeyed!   And I encourage you to start today. In fact, when the Sabbath comes this week, observe it!   Spend time in His Word, rest and see what a blessing it is.   Try skipping the bacon with your eggs for breakfast.   His Torah is a blessing, liberty and the Way our Messiah, Yeshua, walked and lived His life.

Shalom (Peace and wholeness).

For video teachings, blogs, podcasts and other books by Michael Dowis, please visit:

www.michaeldsofer.com